# English

## Age 5-6

# Contents

## Activities

## Quick Tests

## Lynn Huggins-Cooper and Louis Fidge

# Speaking and listening – asking questions

Are you good at listening?
Let's find out!

**1** Ask a grown-up these questions. Can you remember the answers afterwards?

a What was your favourite toy when you were little?

b What was your favourite book?

c Did you have a favourite food?

d Where did you like playing?

e Who was your best friend?

**2** Ask a friend these questions. Can you remember the answers afterwards?

a What do you like best about school?

b What is your favourite activity?

c What do you do at lunchtime?

d What do you play at playtime?

e What do you do after school?

# Rhyming words

Look at this sentence. All the words in bold rhyme. That means the endings of the words have the **same sound**. They all end in the letters *at*.

The **fat cat sat** on the **mat**, watching a **bat**!

**1** Draw a line to join each word with its rhyme partner.

a  can          red

b  pink         sack

c  bug          dot

d  bed          stink

e  pot          plug

f  back         fan

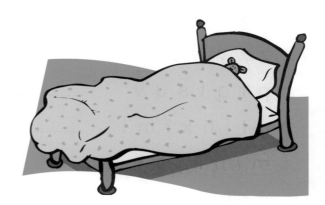

**2** Look in the box to find words that rhyme with each word below. Write the words in the blank spaces.

a  yell    _____

b  dark    _____

c  dog     _____

d  box     _____

e  win     _____

f  sock    _____

g  big     _____

fox
frog
dig
smell
rock
bin
park

# The alphabet

## a b c d e f g h i j k l m n o p q r s t u v w x y z

When words are in **alphabetical order** it means they appear in the same order as the alphabet. *A* words come first, then *b* words, right up until the end of the alphabet.

**bat zebra ant** put into alphabetical order is **ant bat zebra**.

**1** Write these letters in alphabetical order.

a  f b a d c e g  _____

b  z x y w v u  _____

c  p r q t s u v  _____

d  g f i h k j m l  _____

e  m l n k j o p  _____

f  s t v u w r x  _____

g  d f e h i g j k  _____

**2** Write each set of words in alphabetical order.

a  cat    egg    box    _____

b  bag    dig    apple    _____

c  cup    art    dig    _____

d  car    baby    dog    _____

e  wall    bed    door    _____

f  book    sun    leg    _____

g  tree    bird    peg    _____

# Spelling simple words

Learning to spell is easy when you use:
**LOOK, COVER, WRITE, CHECK**.

First **look** at the word. Look to see if there are any letters with tails that hang below the line, or sticks that 'stick up' above the line. Try to see the word in your head.

tail y      | — stick

Then **cover** the word up and try to **write** it. Uncover the word and **check** it. See if you were right. Keep practising!

**1** Learn these words. Use LOOK, COVER, WRITE, CHECK.

a saw    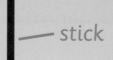    d yes    g was

b say    e did    h but

c now    f not    i run

**2** Look at the picture and add the missing letter to each word. Use the letters in the box to help you.

a m___n        e d___t    ●

b f___n        f w___g

|   |
|---|
| a |
| i |
| o |
| u |

c c___t        g s___n

d p___n        h b___ll

## Writing practice

It is important to **write neatly**, so that people can read your writing. Before you start, make sure you are sitting comfortably and you are holding your pencil in the right way between your finger and thumb.

**1** Trace over these words. Start at the red dot each time.

a way  us  to

b too  how  her

c him  old  one

d or  out  saw

e so  not  now

**2** Copy each word three times.

a see _____ _____ _____

b ran _____ _____ _____

c our _____ _____ _____

d pot _____ _____ _____

e that _____ _____ _____

# Full stops and capital letters

A sentence always **starts** with a capital letter and most sentences **end** with a full stop. The pronoun *I* is always a capital letter.

It is hot today.

/ capital letter     full stop

**1** Rewrite these sentences, adding capital letters and full stops.

a  i like you  _____

b  this is my sister  _____

c  sausages are my favourite  _____

d  i am going out  _____

e  i want to read  _____

**2** These sentences are mixed up. Write them out in the correct order. Use a capital letter and a full stop in each sentence.

a  like brother i my

_____

b  dog my walking likes

_____

c  smell the cat food can its

_____

d  eat we sweets

_____

e  wet makes rain you

_____

# Names

The name of a **person** or **place** should **start** with a capital letter.

My cat is called **W**iggy.

I come from **B**righton.

**1** Circle the letters that should be capitals.

a brian

b mrs jones

c andrew

d england

e mr brown

f miss lacey

g london

h mr smith

i france

j janet

k doctor doolittle

l cambridge

m africa

n scotland

**2** Now <u>underline</u> all of the letters that should be capitals in these sentences. Do not forget to add the full stops!

a my friend jamila comes from yorkshire

b my dog is called bertie

c auntie jane lives in edinburgh

d bruce, stella and jodi are my friends

e we sailed down the river thames

f dad's name is john

g i am going on holiday to portugal with my sister sarah

h i went to durham to see the pantomime cinderella

# *ff* words

Words are made when letters and groups of letters are put together. Learning the way that groups of letters are put together helps you to **build new words**.

$$o + f = of \quad o + ff = off$$

The two *ff*s sound different to one *f* on its own.

**1** Look at these letters and groups of letters. Write the words they make in the puffs of smoke.

a flu + ff =

f sti + ff =

b pu + ff =

g mu + ff =

c bu + ff =

h stu + ff =

d cu + ff =

i sta + ff =

e sni + ff =

j whi + ff =

**2** Write the correct *ff* word next to each picture. Use the words in the box to help you.

| muff | cliff | giraffe | puff | whiff | sniff |
|------|-------|---------|------|-------|-------|

a _____

d _____

b _____

e _____

c _____

f _____

9

## *ll* words

Some words end in *ll*. These letters always have a vowel in front of them.

t**all**

**1** Make words using the endings in the ball.

a b <u>*all bull bill bell*</u>

b y_____

c s_____

d c_____

e h_____

f d_____

g f_____

h p_____

i t_____

j w_____

**2** Write the *ll* word for each picture.

a

c

e

___  ___  ___  ___

b

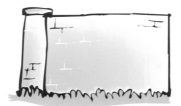

d

f

___  ___  ___  ___

# ss and zz words

Some words end in *ss* or *zz*.

flo**ss**

bu**zz**

**1** Join the *ss* word to the right picture.

a address

b chess

c pass

d dress

e cress

f floss

**2** Choose a word containing *ss* or *zz* from the box to complete each sentence.

| hiss | floss | fuzzy | grass | muzzle | cress |

a I sat on the _____.

b My cat's nose is soft and _____.

c I like egg and _____ sandwiches.

d Candy _____ is sweet!

e My dog wears a _____ when she goes for a walk.

f The snake went _____.

# *bl* words

b and *l* make the letter blend *bl*. Lots of words **start** with *bl*.

**bl**ew

**bl**oom

**1** Tick the words that start with the blend *bl*.

a back dark bland

b black bright big

c baby bin blue

d blend bark brave

e bus blank broom

f bleat bran bill

g burn bleep ball

h bloat bunny barn

i brand bit bleak

j blade brass bust

**2** Draw a picture for each *bl* word. This will show that you know what it means.

a blade

c blow

e blast

b blink

d blue

## ee words

The letters *ee* together sound like someone is squealing!

---

**1** **Draw a line to match each *ee* word to the right picture.**

a sleep

b sheep

c feet

d sleet

e sheet

f bee

g deer

h beep

---

**2** **Draw a circle round the *ee* word in each sentence.**

a The water is deep.

b Have you seen my dad?

c Where have you been?

d My sister is a teenager.

e I shall creep up the stairs, because my brother is sleeping.

f Have a peep at these chicks!

g The car horn went beep.

h In the winter we get sleet as well as snow.

## *oo* sounds

*oo* makes a **special sound**, like an owl hooting.

h**oo**t  r**oo**t  s**oo**n

**1** Draw a picture of the missing *oo* words in the boxes below. Use the words in the box to help you.

| stool | pool | food | school |
|---|---|---|---|

a The cat sat on the _____.

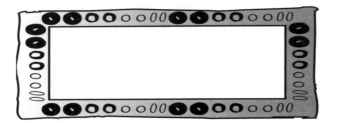

b Who would like to swim in the _____?

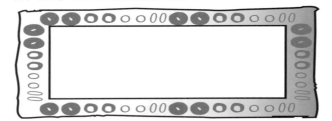

c The _____ was very noisy!

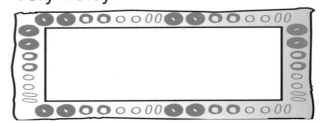

d What is your favourite _____?

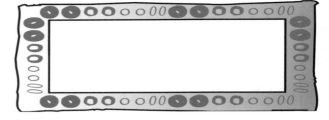

**2** Write the correct *oo* word in each sentence.

a The _____ was bright in the sky.

b The lemonade was lovely and _____.

c I eat yoghurt with a _____.

d Can I come _____?

e _____ is made into jumpers.

too

moon

wool

cool

spoon

# *oa* words

There are lots of words that use the letters *oa* together. They make a sound like the name of the letter *o*.

coach

toad

**1** Which pictures are *oa* words? Circle the ones you choose.

a

c

e

b

d

f

**2** Draw a line to match each *oa* word to its clue.

a toast

b foal

c coal

d loaf

e oak

f boat

g toad

h road

it sails on the sea

cars drive on this

bread

baby horse

it is like a frog

it burns on a fire

a hot, cooked slice of bread

tree

# *ai* words

The letters *a* and *i* blend together to
make the sound *ay* – just like a person
who has not heard what you
said properly!

**1** Draw a picture for each *ai* word.

**a** snail

**c** brain

**e** train

**b** rain

**d** tail

**f** nail

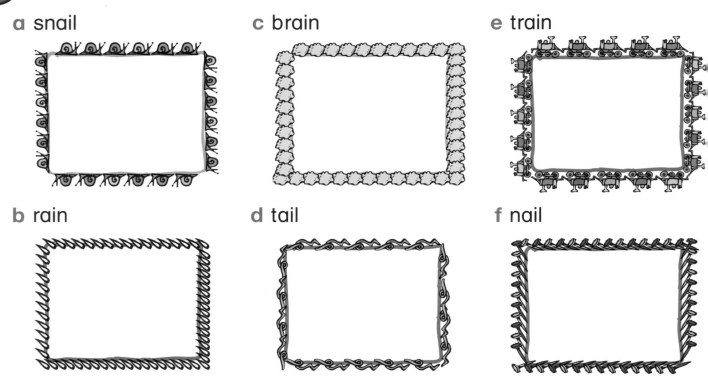

**2** Write a sentence using each *ai* word.

**a** snail _____

**b** main _____

**c** pail _____

**d** fail _____

**e** rain _____

**f** pain _____

# *ie* and *y* words

The letter blend *ie* sometimes makes the same sound as the letter *y*, especially when it is at the end of a word – so it can be confusing!

pie

why

**1** **Which letters are correct? <u>Underline</u> the right answer.**

a  pie   py

b  tie   ty

c  die   dy

d  ly   lie

e  drie   dry

f  try   trie

g  why   whie

h  flie   fly

i  cry   crie

j  by   bie

**2** **Complete the words. They all end in *y* or *ie*.**

a _d_____

c _cr_____

e _t_____

b _fl_____

d _sp_____

# Looking at *un*

*Un* is a **prefix** that can be used at the front of a word to change its meaning. A prefix is a set of letters.

**un** + happy = **un**happy

**1** **Add the *un* to each word to make a new word.**

a   un  +  fair      =   _____

b   un  +  likely    =   _____

c   un  +  aware     =   _____

d   un  +  kind      =   _____

e   un  +  clear     =   _____

f   un  +  wanted    =   _____

**2** <u>Underline</u> **the *un* word in each sentence.**

a   Calling people names is very unkind.

b   Put the unwanted clothes in that bag to go to charity.

c   It is unlikely that an elephant will run across the garden!

d   I think it's unfair that I have to do the dishes.

e   Fighting with my sister makes me unhappy.

# Commas

Commas help us to make sense of the things we read.

When you are reading aloud, commas help you to know when to take a pause.

*The cat went into the garden, but then she changed her mind and came straight back!*

**1** Put the commas in these sentences.

a I like oranges best but I also like apples.

b Would you like this book or would you prefer that one?

c When we get to the shop would you like to buy a cookie?

d Hamsters are my favourite animal but I also love cats.

e I'd like a biscuit but I'd prefer a cake.

**2** Finish these sentences.

a The cat scratched at the window, _____

b It is raining, _____

c The spider crawled up the wall, _____

d I wanted some chocolate, _____

e I saw a shooting star, _____

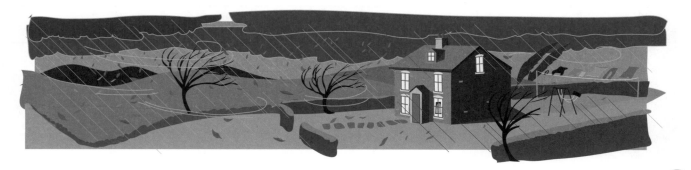

# Exclamation marks

Exclamation marks show strong feelings, such as excitement and shock.

*The dog knocked me over!*

**1** Add the exclamation marks to these sentences.

a I hate cabbage

b I love chocolate cake

c This is the best birthday I have ever had

d What a great book

e Ouch That really hurt

f That was such fun

**2** Write sentences that end in exclamation marks. Remember, they show strong feelings.

a _____

b _____

c _____

d _____

e _____

f _____

# Using *er, est, ed* and *ing*

**Suffixes** are sets of letters that can be added to the end of a word to make a different word.

fast ➡ fast**er** ➡ fast**est**

**1** Add *er* and *est* to these words to make new words.

a slow ➡ _____ _____

b quick ➡ _____ _____

c long ➡ _____ _____

d short ➡ _____ _____

e tall ➡ _____ _____

f strong ➡ _____ _____

**2** Choose the suffix *ed* or *ing* to make sure these sentences make sense.

a The cat jump_____ off the chair.

b It is rain_____.

c The baby laugh_____ when she saw the teddy.

d The mouse keeps squeak_____.

e The sunflower is grow_____ very tall.

f The duck was quack_____ at the chicken.

## Spelling the days of the week

**Monday**   **Tuesday**   **Wednesday**

**Sunday**

**Thursday**   **Friday**   **Saturday**

**1** Learn these spellings. Use LOOK, COVER, WRITE, CHECK.

a Monday _____

b Tuesday _____

c Wednesday _____

d Thursday _____

e Friday _____

f Saturday _____

g Sunday _____

**2** Fill in the missing letters to spell the days of the week.

a Mo_____ _____ay

b Sat_____ _____ _____ay

c T_____u_____s_____a_____

d Tu_____ _____ _____ay

e We_____ _____es_____ _____ _____

f Su_____ _____ _____y

g Fr_____ _____ _____y

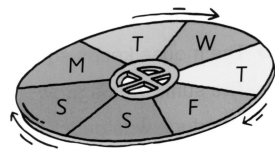

# Plurals

With some words, to change from one thing to more than one thing (a **plural**) you just add an *s*.

With some words you add *es*.

wish ➡ wish**es**

cat ➡ cat**s**

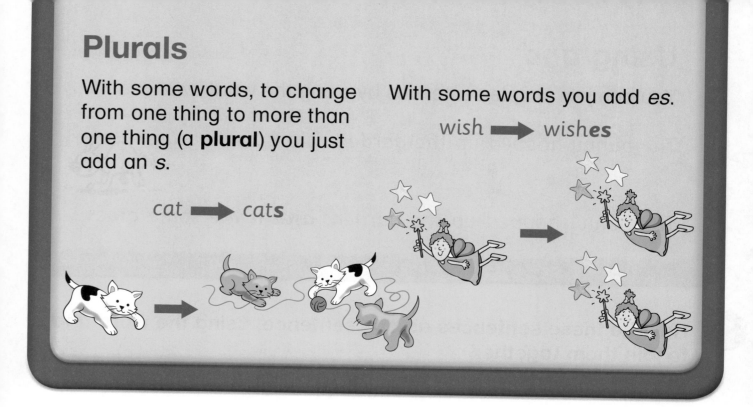

**1** Change these words to plurals.

a rabbit ➡ _____

b dog ➡ _____

c cow ➡ _____

d horse ➡ _____

e chicken ➡ _____

f duck ➡ _____

**2** Change these words to plurals.

a fox ➡ _____

b dish ➡ _____

c class ➡ _____

d kiss ➡ _____

e princess ➡ _____

f dress ➡ _____

# Using *and*

You can join simple sentences by using the word *and*.

*The bunny hopped up the garden. It ate some grass.*

*The bunny hopped up the garden,* **and** *it ate some grass.*

**1** Rewrite these sentences as one sentence, using the word *and* to join them together.

a A moth flew near the window. It patted the glass with its wings.

_____

b My mum likes cake. She likes biscuits.

_____

c My teddy is big. He has long fur.

_____

d The wizard waved his wand. The cat turned into a tiger!

_____

e The cake is chocolate flavour. It has creamy icing.

_____

**2** Draw a line to join the two parts of the sentences together so they make sense.

a I like reading books        1 and a sandpit in the park.

b I like lollies        2 and I like ice cream!

c I went to London        3 and a dog.

d I have a cat        4 and a skateboard.

e There is a swing        5 and watching films.

f I have a bike        6 and to Brighton.

# Contractions

When you see a word like *I'm,* it is called a **contraction**. The apostrophe shows that letters are missing.

## I'm didn't she's

**1** Draw a line to join the words to their contractions.

a will not          he's

b shall not          won't

c I have          I've

d can not          shan't

e he has          can't

**2** Change these words to their contractions.

a did not  _____

b had not  _____

c have not  _____

d I would  _____

e do not _____

# Making words

You can **build words** by adding different groups of letters together.

$$cr + isp = crisp$$

**1** Add these groups of letters together and write the words you make. The first one has been done for you.

**a** th + at = _that_

**b** th + is = _____

**c** th + en = _____

**d** wh + at = _____

**e** wh + en = _____

**f** wh + ip = _____

**g** tr + ap = _____

**h** dr + op = _____

**i** cr + op = _____

**j** br + an = _____

**2** Join together the groups of letters with a line to make words. Use a different colour felt pen for each word.

**a** tr          ant

**b** pl          ade

**c** br          ing

**d** bl          it

**e** cr          en

**f** sm          ab

**g** spl          esh

**h** dr          ile

**i** fr          ip

**j** wh          ee

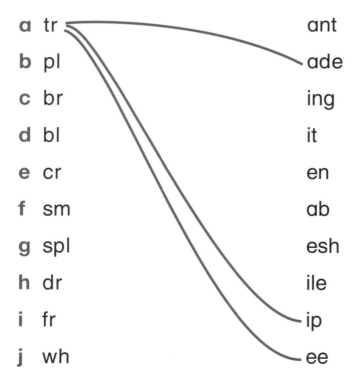

# Syllables

Syllables are the sounds that make up words.

*badger* is made up of **badg + er**

**1** How many syllables are there in each of these animal words? Say the words out loud to help you. Write the number of syllables in the box.

a fox

b robin

c spider

d hedgehog

e squirrel

**2** Break each word into syllables. The first one has been done for you.

a raining ➡ *rain/ing*

b sunshine ➡ _____

c windy ➡ _____

d snowing ➡ _____

e thundering ➡ _____

# In the past

When the **action word** in a sentence ends in *ed* it means the action happened in the past.

*I walked to school yesterday.*

**1** Change the action word to the past tense. The first one has been done for you.

a I enjoy__ed__ the games best.

b I talk_____ to my friend.

c I look_____ at the picture.

d She play_____ with her brother.

e He paint_____ a picture.

f I call_____ my sister.

g They wash_____ their hands.

**2** Write the correct present tense word next to the past tense word. The first one has been done for you.

a jumped ____jump____

b laughed _____

c enjoyed _____

d called _____

e guessed _____

f lifted _____

g watched _____

h worked _____

i helped _____

watch   jump   laugh   help
enjoy   guess   call   work   lift

# Vowels

The letters

## a e i o u

are called **vowels**.

Sometimes *y* acts as a vowel in words like *cry* and *why*.

Do have some tea.

**1** Circle the vowels in these words.

a cottage

b seaside

c woods

d babies

e school

f computer

g picture

h doctor

i berries

j leaf

**2** Fill in the missing vowels to make these words.

a h_____ _____se

c gl_____ss_____s

e c_____k_____

b b_____ _____ks

d m_____lk

f st_____rs

# Consonants

**Consonants** are all the letters of the alphabet except the vowels *a e i o u*.

The consonants are:

# b c d f g h j k l m n p q r s
# t v w x y z

**1** <u>Underline</u> the consonants in these words.

a  b o a t

b  b a b y

c  m o u s e

d  s a n d

e  s u n s h i n e

f  d e s k

g  p e n c i l

h  s c i s s o r s

i  e n v e l o p e

j  t a b l e

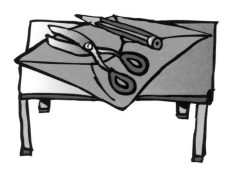

**2** Write the names of the things under the pictures. Use pairs of consonants in the box to help you.

a

___ a ___

c

___ e ___

e

___ a ___

b

___ a ___

d

___ a ___

ct  lg  mn
jm  cn

# Question marks

**Question marks** look like this **?** They are used at the end of a sentence to show it is a question.

Some words give us a clue that a question is being asked:

What...? When...? How...?
Why...? Who...?

Where is my hat?

---

**1** Add a question mark or a full stop at the end of these sentences.

a Do you like football

b I am glad we are going there

c Can we go now

d May I have one please

e You can play

f This is my dog

g What was that noise

h What time is it

**2** Write questions of your own using the words *what, when, how, why, who*. Do not forget the question mark!

a _____

_____

b _____

_____

c _____

_____

d _____

_____

e _____

_____

# Test 1 The alphabet

All **words** are made up of **letters**. There are **26** letters in the **alphabet**.

**Fill in the missing letters.**

Colour in your score

# Test 2 Making some words (1)

The sound of the **first letter** of each of these words is the **same**.

sun        saw        sink

Choose one of these letters to start each word.

**m     p     h**

1. ___eg

6. ___ut

2. ___an

7. ___en

3. ___op

8. ___op

4. ___in

9. ___ug

5. ___at

10. ___en

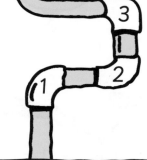

Colour in your score

# Test 3 Making some words (2)

We use **letters** to make **words**.

b + a + t = bat

Do these sums. Write the words you make.

1. s + a + d = _____

6. f + o + x = _____

2. d + i + g = _____

7. n + e + t = _____

3. b + a + g = _____

8. t + u + b = _____

4. t + o + p = _____

9. d + o + g = _____

5. l + e + g = _____

10. j + u + g = _____

Colour in your score

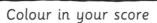

34

# Test 4 Labels

Many pictures have **labels** to help you.

Write the correct name under each animal.

| | | | | |
|---|---|---|---|---|
| monkey | goat | horse | tiger | kangaroo |
| donkey | bear | zebra | camel | panda |

1. _____

2. _____

3. _____

4. _____

5. _____

6. _____

7. _____

8. _____

9. _____

10. _____

Colour in your score

10
9
8
7
6
5
4
3
2
1

# Test 5 **Sentences**

A **sentence** must make **sense**.

I to hop like. ☒    I like to hop. ☑

**Write the words in order to make some sentences.**

1. sun yellow.  The is _____

2. green.  is grass The _____

3. read.  like to I _____

4. lay eggs.  Hens _____

5. lion A roar.  can _____

6. raining.  is It _____

7. in You water.  swim _____

8. ball.  You a kick _____

9. door The shut.  is _____

10. stripes.  A has tiger _____

10

9

8

7

6

5

4

3

2

1

Colour in your score

36

# Test 6 Missing words

A **sentence** must make **sense**.

ROAR

A roars. ☒          A lion roars. ☑

**Choose the best word to finish each sentence.**

| | | | | |
|---|---|---|---|---|
| elephant | sun | money | cup | kangaroo |
| banana | star | spade | bike | umbrella |

1. You ride a _____.

2. The _____ shines.

3. A _____ twinkles.

4. You spend _____.

5. You eat a _____.

6. A _____ hops.

7. You need an _____ in the rain.

8. You drink from a _____.

9. An _____ has a trunk.

10. You dig with a _____.

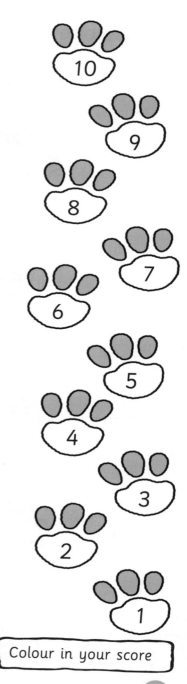

10
9
8
7
6
5
4
3
2
1

Colour in your score

37

# Test 7 Last letters

The sound of the **last letter** of each of these words is the **same**.

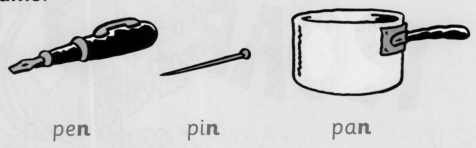

pen       pin       pan

**Choose one of these letters to finish each word.**

t     g     p

1. ba____

2. ma____

3. zi____

4. cu____

5. ha____

6. wi____

7. ne____

8. do____

9. ru____

10. po____

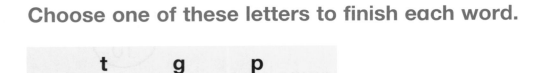

Colour in your score

# Test 8 Groups of words

We sometimes **group** words together. These are all **birds**.

hen          parrot        sparrow

bike        rocket      helicopter        bus        aeroplane

boat        yacht         car           ship          lorry

**Sort these things into groups.**

Things that go on land.

| | |
|---|---|
| 1. _____ | 3. _____ |
| 2. _____ | 4. _____ |

Things that fly in the sky.     Things that go on the water.

| | |
|---|---|
| 5. _____ | 8. _____ |
| 6. _____ | 9. _____ |
| 7. _____ | 10. _____ |

Colour in your score

# Test 9 **Word building**

We can **build** words from **letters** and **groups of letters**.

b + ag

bag

r + ag

rag

w + ag

wag

**Do these sums. Write the words you make.**

**1.** f + an = _____

**2.** s + ix = _____

**3.** v + an = _____

**4.** n + od = _____

**5.** l + eg = _____

**6.** r + od = _____

**7.** p + eg = _____

**8.** c + ut = _____

**9.** m + ix = _____

**10.** n + ut = _____

10
9
8
7
6
5
4
3
2
1

Colour in your score

# Test 10 Middle letters

The sound of the **middle letter** of each of these words is the **same**.

pan   bat  bag

**Choose the correct middle letter to make each word.**

| a | o | o | i |
|---|---|---|---|
| 1. j__m | | 6. s__b | |

| u | a | i | e |
|---|---|---|---|
| 2. t__p | | 7. t__n | |

| u | o | e | i |
|---|---|---|---|
| 3. l__g | | 8. t__n | |

| o | u | a | i |
|---|---|---|---|
| 4. b__n | | 9. b__b | |

| u | e | e | a |
|---|---|---|---|
| 5. t__b | | 10. j__t | |

Colour in your score

# Test 11 Capital letters and full stops

A **sentence** always begins with a **capital letter** and often ends with a **full stop**.

*The girl fell off her bike!*

**Write these sentences correctly.**

1. the rain falls _____

2. a tree grows tall _____

3. the sky is blue _____

4. my cup is full _____

5. a cow moos _____

6. we like books _____

7. you bang a drum _____

8. it is sunny _____

9. a ball is round _____

10. i like to sing _____

10
9
8
7
6
5
4
3
2
1

Colour in your score

42

# Test 12 The letters *ff*, *ll*, *zz* and *ss*

Some words end with **double letters**.

Pa**ss** the ba**ll**.

| | doll | off | bell | |
|---|---|---|---|---|
| hill | | buzz | puff | fall |
| | hiss | fuzz | fuss | |

**Write the words that end with *ss*.**

1. _____  2. _____

**Write the words that end with *ll*.**

3. _____  5. _____

4. _____  6. _____

**Write the words that end with *zz*.**

7. _____  8. _____

**Write the words that end with *ff*.**

9. _____  10. _____

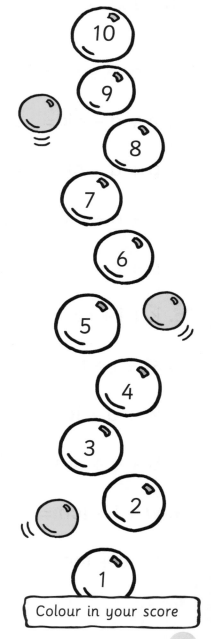

Colour in your score

# Test 13 The letters *ck* and *tch*

Many words end in *ck* or *tch*.

A du**ck** says qua**ck**.

The wi**tch** has an i**tch**.

**Do these sums. Write the words you make.**

1. b + a + ck = _____

2. p + a + ck = _____

3. n + e + ck = _____

4. p + e + ck = _____

5. k + i + ck = _____

6. st + i + tch = _____

7. w + a + tch = _____

8. b + a + tch _____

9. w + i + tch = _____

10. f + e + tch + _____

10
9
8
7
6
5
4
3
2
1

Colour in your score

44

# Test 14 The letters *ng* and *nk*

Many words end in *ng* and *nk*.

I can si**ng**.

I can thi**nk**.

Find and write the *ng* or *nk* words that are hiding.

1. a(b a n g)w    __bang__

2. b a n k t y    _____

3. h g k i n g    _____

4. b s o n g m    _____

5. f v s a n k    _____

6. h a n g j b    _____

7. s a r i n g    _____

8. z l i n k n    _____

9. b u n k x c    _____

10. j h p i n k    _____

10

9

8

7

6

5

4

3

2

1

Colour in your score

# Test 15 Letter blends at the beginning of words

These words all have *l* as a second letter.

slide      fly      clock     black     glue

**Write the new words you make.**

1. Change the **fl** in **fl**ip to **sl**.    _slip_

2. Change the **pl** in **pl**ot to **sl**. _____

3. Change the **sl** in **sl**at to **fl**. _____

4. Change the **cl** in **cl**ick to **fl**. _____

5. Change the **fl** in **fl**ap to **cl**. _____

6. Change the **bl** in **bl**ink to **cl**. _____

7. Change the **cl** in **cl**ot to **bl**. _____

8. Change the **sl** in **sl**ack to **bl**. _____

9. Change the **cl** in **cl**ass to **gl**. _____

10. Change the **cl** in **cl**ad to **gl**. _____

10

9

8

7

6

5

4

3

2

1

Colour in your score

46

# Test 16 Letter blends at the end of words

Say these words slowly. Listen to the way they **end**.

bo**lt**    she**lf**    mi**lk**    he**lp**    go**ld**

| | hold | elf | milk | |
|---|---|---|---|---|
| yelp | belt | silk | gold |
| | help | shelf | melt | |

**Write the pairs of rhyming words.**

**Write the words that end with** *ld*.

1. _____    2. _____

**Write the words that end with** *lf*.

3. _____    4. _____

**Write the words that end with** *lk*.

5. _____    6. _____

**Write the words that end with** *lp*.

7. _____    8. _____

**Write the words that end with** *lt*.

9. _____    10. _____

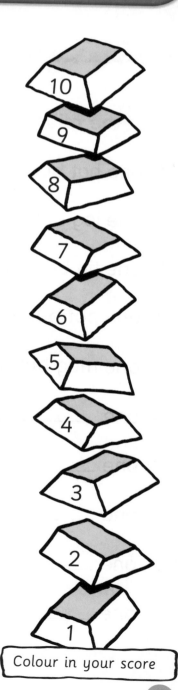

10
9
8
7
6
5
4
3
2
1

Colour in your score

# Test 17 **Plurals**

**Plural** means when there is **more than one**.

We add *s* to many words to make them plural.

one rabbit

three rabbit**s**

**Fill in the missing word.**

1. one hat but two _____

2. one leg but two _____

3. one tin but two _____

4. one pot but two _____

5. one mug but two _____

6. one _____ but two pans

7. one _____ but two pets

8. one _____ but two lips

9. one _____ but two dogs

10. one _____ but two sums

Colour in your score

# Test 18 **Sets of words**

This is a **set** of fruit.

orange   banana   apple

This is a **set** of animals.

lion      monkey    elephant

potato   butterfly  cabbage  onion   ant

carrot    beetle   cauliflower  earwig    turnip

**Write the names of the vegetables.**

1. _____        4. _____

2. _____        5. _____

3. _____        6. _____

**Write the names of the insects.**

7. _____        9. _____

8. _____       10. _____

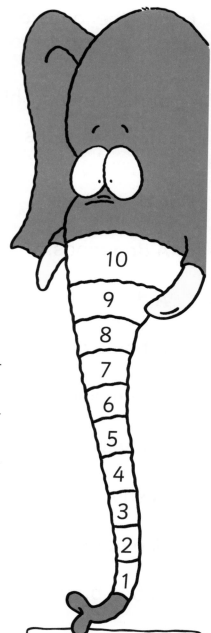

| 10 |
| 9 |
| 8 |
| 7 |
| 6 |
| 5 |
| 4 |
| 3 |
| 2 |
| 1 |

Colour in your score

# Test 19 Silly sentences

A **sentence** must make **sense**.

The dog moos. ☒    The dog barks. ☑

Change the last word so that each sentence makes sense. Choose words from the box to help you.

| | | | | |
|---|---|---|---|---|
| barks | moos | hisses | cheeps | neighs |
| chirps | quacks | bleats | brays | buzzes |

1. A cow barks. _____

2. A dog moos. _____

3. A duck hisses. _____

4. A horse cheeps. _____

5. A hen neighs. _____

6. A sheep chirps. _____

7. A snake quacks. _____

8. A bird bleats. _____

9. A bee brays. _____

10. A donkey buzzes. _____

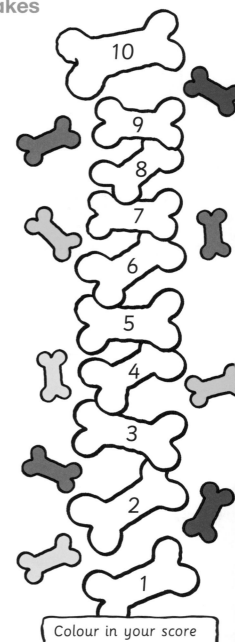

Colour in your score

# Test 20 **The letters *sh* and *ch***

You will find *sh* and *ch* in many words.

fi**sh** and **ch**ips

**Choose *sh* or *ch* to complete each word.**

1. _____est

2. _____ell

3. _____ip

4. di_____

5. _____eep

6. ben_____

7. _____icken

8. tor_____

9. _____eese

10. bru_____

Colour in your score

# Test 21 The letters *ee* and *oo*

The letters *ee* and *oo* are two common letter patterns.

I have some b**oo**ts on my f**ee**t.

Choose *ee* or *oo* to complete each word.

1. _____l

2. st_____l

3. p_____l

4. br_____m

5. m_____n

6. tr_____

7. w_____p

8. f_____d

9. sw_____t

10. b_____

Colour in your score

52

# Test 22 The letters *ay* and *ai*

The letters *ay* often come at the **end** of a word.

The letters *ai* often come in the **middle** of a word.

tr**ay**

tr**ai**n

**Choose *ai* or *ay* to complete the word in each sentence.**

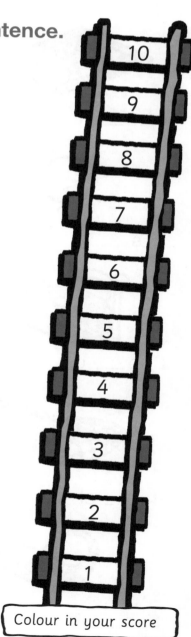

1. It is a lovely d_____.

2. The r_____n is falling.

3. I hit the n_____l with a hammer.

4. You can swim in the b_____.

5. You can make things with cl_____.

6. The sn_____l went slowly.

7. I had to w_____t for my dinner.

8. You can pl_____ in the park.

9. The plates are on a tr_____.

10. You will have to w_____t and see.

10
9
8
7
6
5
4
3
2
1

Colour in your score

# Test 23 Vowels and consonants

There are **26** letters in the **alphabet**.

| a | b | c | d | e | f | g | h | i | j | k | l | m |
|---|---|---|---|---|---|---|---|---|---|---|---|---|
| n | o | p | q | r | s | t | u | v | w | x | y | z |

The five **vowels** are a, e, i, o, u.

All the other letters are called **consonants**.

**Fill in the missing letter in each word.**

1. m____t

2. s____n

3. b____d

4. ____et

5. b____b

6. b____g

7. fo____

**6**

8. s____x

9. m____d

10. bu____

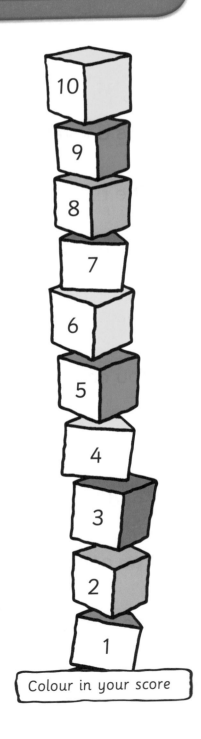

10
9
8
7
6
5
4
3
2
1

Colour in your score

54

## Test 24 Names

Whenever we write **someone's name** we should always **start** with a **capital letter**.

Humpty Dumpty sat on a wall.

**Write the names of these nursery rhyme characters correctly.**

1. humpty dumpty  _____

2. little bo peep  _____

3. margery daw  _____

4. tommy tucker  _____

5. jack horner  _____

6. polly  _____

7. mary  _____

8. lucy locket  _____

9. georgie porgie  _____

10. bobby shafto  _____

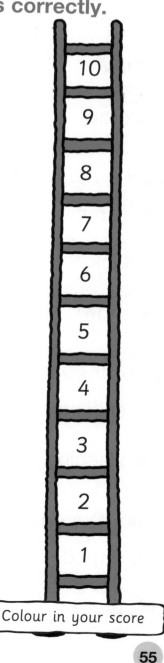

Colour in your score

10
9
8
7
6
5
4
3
2
1

55

# Test 25 **The endings *ing* and *ed***

We can add *ing* and *ed* to the ends of some words.

I am wash**ing** my face.
wash + ing = washing

Yesterday I wash**ed** my feet.
wash + ed = washed

**Add *ing* to each word. Write the word you make.**

1. talk _____

2. lick _____

3. draw _____

**Add *ed* to each word. Write the word you make.**

4. shout _____

5. kick _____

6. crawl _____

**Take the *ing* off. Write the word you are left with.**

7. sniffing _____

8. sleeping _____

**Take the *ed* off. Write the word you are left with.**

9. turned _____

10. passed _____

Colour in your score

56

# Test 26 **Questions**

A question must begin with a **capital letter** and end with a **question mark**.

capital letter

question mark

How many legs has a spider?

**Write these questions correctly.**

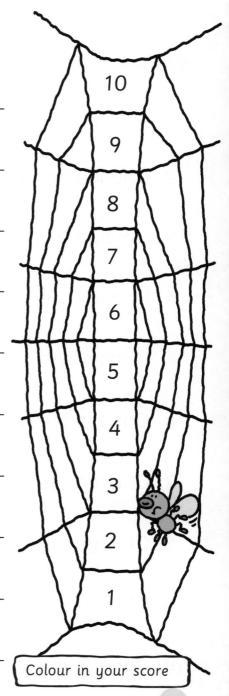

1. what is for tea

   _____

2. when are you coming

   _____

3. what shape is a ball

   _____

4. who is making that noise

   _____

5. where do you live

   _____

6. how many sweets have you got

   _____

7. what is your address

   _____

8. who is your teacher

   _____

9. when is it time for dinner

   _____

10. where is London

   _____

10
9
8
7
6
5
4
3
2
1

Colour in your score

# Test 27 The letters *ea* and *oa*

The two letter patterns *ea* and *oa* are common.

a b**oa**t on the s**ea**

Write the new words you make.

1. Change the **s** in s**ea** to **t**. _____

2. Change the **b** in **b**eat to **s**. _____

3. Change the **l** in **l**eap to **h**. _____

4. Change the **b** in **b**eak to **l**. _____

5. Change the **t** in **t**each to **b**. _____

6. Change the **g** in **g**oat to **b**. _____

7. Change the **f** in **f**oal to **g**. _____

8. Change the **t** in **t**oad to **r**. _____

9. Change the **c** in **c**oast to **t**. _____

10. Change the **p** in **p**oach to **c**. _____

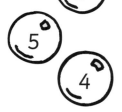

Colour in your score

58

# Test 28 **Magic *e***

Look what happens when we add *e* to the **end** of some words.

hop + e = hop**e**

**Do these sums. Write the words you make.**

1. mad + e =  _____

2. slid + e =  _____

3. plan + e =  _____

4. can + e =  _____

5. cub + e =  _____

6. rob + e =  _____

7. shin + e =  _____

8. cut + e =  _____

9. tap + e =  _____

10. bit + e =  _____

Colour in your score

# Test 29 The months of the year

It is important to know how to spell the **months of the year** correctly.

Here are the months of the year in the wrong order.

| | | | |
|---|---|---|---|
| August | May | December | January |
| February | June | October | March |
| September | April | November | July |

Fill in the missing months in order. Spell them correctly.
The first two months have been done for you.

January

February

1. _____

2. _____

3. _____

4. _____

5. _____

6. _____

7. _____

8. _____

9. _____

10. _____

Colour in your score

60

# Test 30 Rhyming

Sometimes words that rhyme use the same spelling pattern.

A plane can **fly** in the **sky**.

| | ring | bake | train | |
|---|---|---|---|---|
| goat | | cool | king | coat |
| | chain | pool | cake | |

**Write the pairs of rhyming words.**

**Write the *ing* words.**

1. _____

2. _____

**Write the *ain* words.**

7. _____

8. _____

**Write the *ool* words.**

3. _____

4. _____

**Write the *ake* words.**

9. _____

10. _____

**Write the *oat* words.**

5. _____

6. _____

Colour in your score

61

# ANSWERS

## Page 2

**1.** Make sure your child can ask the questions successfully, and can remember the answers afterwards.

**2.** Make sure your child can ask the questions successfully, and can remember their friend's answers afterwards.

## Page 3

**1.**
| | |
|---|---|
| **a** fan | **d** red |
| **b** stink | **e** dot |
| **c** plug | **f** sack |

**2.**
| | |
|---|---|
| **a** smell | **e** bin |
| **b** park | **f** rock |
| **c** frog | **g** dig |
| **d** fox | |

## Page 4

**1.**
**a** a b c d e f g
**b** u v w x y z
**c** p q r s t u v
**d** f g h i j k l m
**e** j k l m n o p
**f** r s t u v w x
**g** d e f g h i j k

**2.**
**a** box, cat, egg
**b** apple, bag, dig
**c** art, cup, dig
**d** baby, car, dog
**e** bed, door, wall
**f** book, leg, sun
**g** bird, peg, tree

## Page 5

**1.** Spellings remembered.

**2.**
**a** man
**b** fan/fin/fun
**c** cat/cot/cut
**d** pan/pin/pun
**e** dot
**f** wag/wig
**g** sin/son/sun
**h** ball/bill/bull

## Page 6

**1.** Words overwritten neatly.

**2.** Words copied correctly; rounded letters, correctly formed, sitting on lines.

## Page 7

**1.**
**a** I like you.
**b** This is my sister.
**c** Sausages are my favourite.
**d** I am going out.
**e** I want to read.

**2.**
**a** I like my brother.
**b** My dog likes walking.
**c** The cat can smell its food.
**d** We eat sweets.
**e** Rain makes you wet.

## Page 8

**1.**
**a** Ⓑrian
**b** Ⓜrs Ⓙones
**c** Ⓐndrew
**d** Ⓔngland
**e** Ⓜr Ⓑrown
**f** Ⓜiss Ⓛacey
**g** Ⓛondon
**h** Ⓜr Ⓢmith
**i** Ⓕrance
**j** Ⓙanet
**k** Ⓓoctor Ⓓoolittle
**l** Ⓒambridge
**m** Ⓐfrica
**n** Ⓢcotland

**2.**
**a** My friend <u>J</u>amila comes from <u>Y</u>orkshire.
**b** My dog is called <u>B</u>ertie.
**c** Auntie <u>J</u>ane lives in <u>E</u>dinburgh.
**d** <u>B</u>ruce, <u>S</u>tella and <u>J</u>odi are my friends.
**e** <u>W</u>e sailed down the <u>R</u>iver <u>T</u>hames.
**f** <u>D</u>ad's name is <u>J</u>ohn.
**g** <u>I</u> am going on holiday to <u>P</u>ortugal with my sister <u>S</u>arah.
**h** <u>I</u> went to <u>D</u>urham to see the pantomime <u>C</u>inderella.

## Page 9

**1.**
| | |
|---|---|
| **a** fluff | **f** stiff |
| **b** puff | **g** muff |
| **c** buff | **h** stuff |
| **d** cuff | **i** staff |
| **e** sniff | **j** whiff |

**2.**
| | |
|---|---|
| **a** giraffe | **d** whiff |
| **b** puff | **e** cliff |
| **c** sniff | **f** muff |

## Page 10

**1.** Children will not know all of the words below, but they are given for correctness.
**a** ball, bull, bill, bell
**b** yell
**c** sill, sell
**d** call, cell, cull

**e** hill, hall, hull, hell
**f** doll, dell, dull, dill
**g** fall, fill, full, fell
**h** pull, pill, pall, poll
**i** till, tall, tell, toll
**j** will, wall, well

**2.**
| | |
|---|---|
| **a** ball | **d** bull |
| **b** wall | **e** well |
| **c** bell | **f** doll |

## Page 11

**1.**

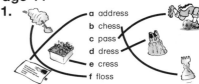

**2.**
| | |
|---|---|
| **a** grass | **d** floss |
| **b** fuzzy | **e** muzzle |
| **c** cress | **f** hiss |

## Page 12

**1.**
| | |
|---|---|
| **a** bland | **f** bleat |
| **b** black | **g** bleep |
| **c** blue | **h** bloat |
| **d** blend | **i** bleak |
| **e** blank | **j** blade |

**2.** Check child's pictures of the words listed.

## Page 13

**1.**

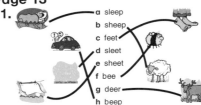

**2.**
**a** deep
**b** seen
**c** been
**d** teenager
**e** creep, sleeping
**f** peep
**g** beep
**h** sleet

## Page 14

**1.** Pictures of the items mentioned:
| | |
|---|---|
| **a** stool | **c** school |
| **b** pool | **d** food |

**2.**
| | |
|---|---|
| **a** moon | **d** too |
| **b** cool | **e** Wool |
| **c** spoon | |

**Page 15**
1. Circled: a, d, e, f
2. **a** a hot, cooked slice of bread
   **b** baby horse
   **c** it burns on a fire
   **d** bread
   **e** tree
   **f** it sails on the sea
   **g** it is like a frog
   **h** cars drive on this

**Page 16**
1. Check child's pictures of the items listed.
2. Sentences using the words listed.

**Page 17**
1. **a** pie  **e** dry  **h** fly
   **b** tie  **f** try  **i** cry
   **c** die  **g** why  **j** by
   **d** lie
2. **a** die  **c** cry  **e** tie
   **b** fly  **d** spy

**Page 18**
1. **a** unfair  **d** unkind
   **b** unlikely  **e** unclear
   **c** unaware  **f** unwanted
2. **a** unkind  **d** unfair
   **b** unwanted  **e** unhappy
   **c** unlikely

**Page 19**
1. **a** I like oranges best, but I also like apples.
   **b** Would you like this book, or would you prefer that one?
   **c** When we get to the shop, would you like to buy a cookie?
   **d** Hamsters are my favourite animal, but I also love cats.
   **e** I'd like a biscuit, but I'd prefer a cake.
2. Any sensible, meaningful sentence endings.

**Page 20**
1. Talk to your child about why there are exclamation marks at the end of each sentence.
2. Any sensible sentences that end in exclamation marks. Again, talk to your child about why exclamation marks need to be included.

**Page 21**
1. **a** slower, slowest
   **b** quicker, quickest
   **c** longer, longest
   **d** shorter, shortest
   **e** taller, tallest
   **f** stronger, strongest
2. **a** jumped  **d** squeaking
   **b** raining  **e** growing
   **c** laughed  **f** quacking

**Page 22**
1. Check your child has learnt the correct spellings.
2. **a** Monday  **e** Wednesday
   **b** Saturday  **f** Sunday
   **c** Thursday  **g** Friday
   **d** Tuesday

**Page 23**
1. **a** rabbits  **d** horses
   **b** dogs  **e** chickens
   **c** cows  **f** ducks
2. **a** foxes  **d** kisses
   **b** dishes  **e** princesses
   **c** classes  **f** dresses

**Page 24**
1. **a** A moth flew near the window, and it patted the glass with its wings.
   **b** My mum likes cake, and she likes biscuits.
   **c** My teddy is big, and he has long fur.
   **d** The wizard waved his wand, and the cat turned into a tiger!
   **e** The cake is chocolate flavour, and it has creamy icing.
2. **a** 5  **c** 6  **e** 1
   **b** 2  **d** 3  **f** 4

**Page 25**
1. **a** won't  **d** can't
   **b** shan't  **e** he's
   **c** I've
2. **a** didn't  **d** I'd
   **b** hadn't  **e** don't
   **c** haven't

**Page 26**
1. **a** that  **f** whip
   **b** this  **g** trap
   **c** then  **h** drop
   **d** what  **i** crop
   **e** when  **j** bran
2. Words created using word beginnings and endings.
   **a** trade, trip, tree
   **b** plant
   **c** bring

**d** blade, blab, blip (bling, if the child knows this word)
**e** crab
**f** smile
**g** split
**h** drab, drip
**i** fresh, free
**j** when, while, whip, whee

**Page 27**
1. **a** 1  **c** 2  **e** 2
   **b** 2  **d** 2
2. **a** rain/ing  **d** snow/ing
   **b** sun/shine  **e** thun/der/ing
   **c** win/dy

**Page 28**
1. **a** enjoyed  **e** painted
   **b** talked  **f** called
   **c** looked  **g** washed
   **d** played
2. **a** jump  **f** lift
   **b** laugh  **g** watch
   **c** enjoy  **h** work
   **d** call  **i** help
   **e** guess

**Page 29**
1. **a** c o t t a g e
   **b** s e a s i d e
   **c** w o o d s
   **d** b a b i e s
   **e** s c h o o l
   **f** c o m p u t e r
   **g** p i c t u r e
   **h** d o c t o r
   **i** b e r r i e s
   **j** l e a f
2. **a** house  **d** milk
   **b** books  **e** cake
   **c** glasses  **f** stars

**Page 30**
1. **a** boat  **f** desk
   **b** baby  **g** pencil
   **c** mouse  **h** scissors
   **d** sand  **i** envelope
   **e** sunshine  **j** table
2. **a** cat  **c** leg  **e** man
   **b** jam  **d** can

**Page 31**
1. **a** ?  **d** ?  **g** ?
   **b** .  **e** .  **h** ?
   **c** ?  **f** .
2. Questions written using the question words provided.

# ANSWERS

**Page 32**
1. c
2. g
3. i
4. m
5. p
6. s
7. t
8. v
9. x
10. z

**Page 33**
1. peg
2. pan
3. hop
4. pin
5. mat
6. hut
7. hen
8. mop
9. mug
10. pen

**Page 34**
1. sad
2. dig
3. bag
4. top
5. leg
6. fox
7. net
8. tub
9. dog
10. jug

**Page 35**
1. camel
2. horse
3. kangaroo
4. zebra
5. bear
6. tiger
7. monkey
8. goat
9. donkey
10. panda

**Page 36**
1. The sun is yellow.
2. The grass is green.
3. I like to read.
4. Hens lay eggs.
5. A lion can roar.
6. It is raining.
7. You swim in water.
8. You kick a ball.
9. The door is shut.
10. A tiger has stripes.

**Page 37**
1. bike
2. sun
3. star
4. money
5. banana
6. kangaroo
7. umbrella
8. cup
9. elephant
10. spade

**Page 38**
1. bag
2. map
3. zip
4. cup
5. hat
6. wig
7. net
8. dog
9. rug
10. pot

**Page 39**
Answers 1–4, 5–7, 8–10 can be given in any order.
1. bike
2. bus
3. car
4. lorry
5. rocket
6. helicopter
7. aeroplane
8. boat
9. yacht
10. ship

**Page 40**
1. fan
2. six
3. van
4. nod
5. leg
6. rod
7. peg
8. cut
9. mix
10. nut

**Page 41**
1. jam
2. tap
3. log
4. bun
5. tub
6. sob
7. ten
8. tin
9. bib
10. jet

**Page 42**
1. The rain falls.
2. A tree grows tall.
3. The sky is blue.
4. My cup is full.
5. A cow moos.
6. We like books.
7. You bang a drum.
8. It is sunny.
9. A ball is round.
10. I like to sing.

**Page 43**
Answers 1–2, 3–6, 7–8, 9–10 can be given in any order.
1. hiss
2. fuss
3. doll
4. bell
5. hill
6. fall
7. buzz
8. fuzz
9. off
10. puff

**Page 44**
1. back
2. pack
3. neck
4. peck
5. kick
6. stitch
7. watch
8. batch
9. witch
10. fetch

**Page 45**
1. bang
2. bank
3. king
4. song
5. sank
6. hang
7. ring
8. link
9. bunk
10. pink